DRIVER'S SAFETY
Danger Spot and Speed Manual

J K Glaspy

ATHENA PRESS
LONDON

DRIVER'S SAFETY
Danger Spot and Speed Manual
Copyright © J K Glaspy 2006

All Rights Reserved

ISBN 1 84401 551 3

First Published in 1997 by
MAIN-SAFE AUSTRALIA
Townsville, Queensland
Second Edition 1998
Special Edition 1999

Published in 2006 by
ATHENA PRESS
Queen's House, 2 Holly Road
Twickenham, TW1 4EG
United Kingdom

Printed for Athena Press

In memory of my brother Daryl.

DISCLAIMER

The author and publisher of this manual cannot be held liable for any personal harm or injury, property damage, economic loss, emotional distress or other detriment arising during or as a result of adherence to these suggestions. The reader utilises the suggestions contained herein at their own risk and is under no implied or express obligation to adhere to the views expressed. The manual and the suggestions within it cannot, therefore, be used as an excuse for failing to avoid an accident, and it cannot be used by any individual to excuse or blame a driver for negligence in the event of a collision. The reader, therefore, uses the manual at their own risk and is entirely personally liable for any detrimental consequences resulting from their actions.

CONTENTS

ABOUT THE AUTHOR

I was born in Oxnard, California on 21 October 1960 and migrated to Australia in 1966 with my parents. We travelled around the continent for a year then settled on a dairy farm near Malanda in the Atherton Tablelands. I was schooled in Malanda from 1967 to 1976 then moved to Rockhampton, and after several jobs joined the Queensland Railways as a cleaner then locomotive fireman/driver.

It was during this period, in 1979, that I applied for my first Australian Patent, it being for a railway track switching-point device, called a Three-Way Switching Point. I later applied for an International Patent and proceeded to offer the concept to Australian, American, French and Japanese rail authorities and rail component manufacturers. The patent supersedes the present railway Permanent Way, and to my knowledge has not been superseded or further developed.

Despite it being considered more efficient and to provide faster switching than conventional switch points by local and national manufacturers, I eventually suspended development of the concept. Some opposition to the device from rail authorities, and projected expenses involved in the manufacture and testing of the prototypes, would prove prohibitively expensive without any financial support from State, Federal or International governments.

Superseding the conventional switching-point mechanism of railway and conveyor tracks proved to be a hard act to follow when re-applying my creative talents, and not until 1989 did I again apply for an Australian Patent of such a standard. This time it was for an electrical safety switch, referred to as the Safety-Line Switch. It was offered to Australian manufacturers and retailers, however, even with the documented support from Standards Australia, the Australian Electrical and Electronic Manufacturer's Association and the Queensland Electricity Commission, I have as yet been unable to convince Australian electrical manufacturers of the necessity of the device. It not only supersedes the Australian electrical standard, as stated by several of these authorities, but also has inherent advantages regarding user safety and ongoing reduced conservation of electricity. To my knowledge this patent has not as yet been superseded or developed further either.

During this period I also invented a board game called 'Evasion' and proceeded to offer it to Australian manufacturers during 1985 and 1986. This patented game was not manufactured on a large scale and I have only recently again revisited the concept, and now intend to re-offer it to manufacturers.

I began a tertiary entrance TAFE course in 1991 and in 1992 was offered a place in the arts faculty of the James Cook University in Cairns, which I accepted. In 1992 I moved to Townsville and applied to switch to the law faculty as a joint degree undergraduate, gaining this place in 1994. I have completed two-thirds of the joint degree at present, but I have suspended my studies until I am financially able to return and complete the course.

A copy of the *Driver's Safety: Danger Spot and Speed Manual* was first issued to the National Library of Australia under Australian Copyright legislation in 1997. It was in September of 1996 that I made my first definite decision to produce the book, firstly for my own use then soon after for public release. I started with no real idea whatsoever of what I would include in the text, but simply that I would produce a book which I could refer to, to improve safety levels for my motoring travels. The text went through several changes, and today is quite different to the early editions, which were much larger and less attractive. I believe that the text today is as close to what I set out to produce in the beginning as I can get, and as a result I have decided now to move on to new ideas and to leave the text in its present format.

I did not officially become involved in public safety infrastructure development until I invented the electrical safety switch in 1989. That invention, combined with the earlier railway track patent, eventually instilled within me a binding duty to continue work on safety infrastructure that could benefit the public as a whole. To date my work, therefore, encompasses rail transport efficiency; pleasure and entertainment; public electrical safety; and vehicle driver safety. I intend to continue working within this sphere and hope to devise other public safety infrastructure alternatives in similar areas.

I was married in Rockhampton in 1978 to a local girl and remained married for eleven years. I have two children from that marriage who do not live with me, and at present I am a bachelor. I was naturalised an Australian in 1990 and hold dual citizenship. I reside in a private house in Townsville and intend to stay in the city for the foreseeable future, or until I complete my work and studies here.

James Glaspy, 2006

INTRODUCTION

Today's road-going modes of transport are reminiscent of the horse-drawn stagecoaches of the eighteenth century, and vehicles to date have been largely unable to protect the occupants from serious injury in the event of a collision while travelling at today's recommended speeds. Regardless of claims made in relation to safety, vehicles are simply not built to withstand the elements of their operating environment and cannot effectively protect the occupants from harm in a serious collision with another vehicle, a concrete barrier, objects on or near the road, or rail traffic. The 6 mm thick glass windscreen and the 3 mm door glass provide the driver and occupants with virtually no protection in the event of a serious collision. A reinforced steel cocoon completely surrounding the occupants and extending significantly in all six directions may provide improved protection in a collision, but this type of vehicle is not available. This manual is, therefore, *vitally important* to all vehicle users in enabling them to travel more safely.

This manual covers most vehicles that use public and private access roads, and includes charts to be followed when weather and road conditions change. In particular it covers danger spots where the majority of fatal accidents occur and provides speed charts for approaching these danger-spot areas. When adhered to, the suggested speed limits and operating procedures could constantly improve travel safety. However, this is only a suggested course of action, intended to prolong, protect and preserve the safety of the driver and the occupants and of other road users. The manual is intended to be read thoroughly and the speed limits in the Condition and Speed Charts and the Danger Spot Speed Charts recognised. It is intended to be kept in the vehicle's glove compartment and referred to constantly in all situations.

The safety suggestions charted within the manual are significantly more stringent than other recommendations, and are devised specifically to reduce the possibility of serious harm or injury occurring to the vehicle's occupants. The manual applies to all road jurisdictions, including local, regional, state and federal, and exceeds recommended regulations. However, it is not directly or indirectly linked with any authority besides that of the author. This manual is intended to encourage readers to proceed at reasonable speeds on public roads in order to maintain safety levels; it is a limited guide intended to assist the reader to travel safely.

The manual is divided into various sections, including action to be taken in altered road and weather conditions when travelling in a car or four-wheel-drive; a truck or bus; or a motorcycle. The manual also includes sections on bad visibility; danger spots; places to avoid; day and night and wet and dry weather conditions; various other road conditions; cyclists and pedestrians; fatigue; and general driver safety. Note: References to right or left herein refer to right-hand drive vehicles travelling on the left side of the road, and will be the opposite for left-hand drive vehicles travelling on the right side of the road; and suggested approach speeds at intersections herein refer to drivers travelling through the intersections of main through ways as approaches from secondary access roads will often be much slower.

WEATHER CONDITIONS

Relevant and applicable to all safe vehicle utilisation are weather conditions and the effects these conditions have on danger spots, the road and the vehicle. Any changes in weather conditions will require the driver to take action in accordance with these changes. Drivers may be required to slow down and be physically able to stop and to be visually aware at danger spots and to remain aware of weather changes as they effect the safe operation of the vehicle and may risk the safety of its occupants.

A narrow highway may turn into a slippery trap after a storm on a hot day; an evening drive may turn risky where a wall of fog appears, limiting the driver's visibility and compromising the safety level of the vehicle and its occupants. A blinding glare of sunlight causing temporary loss of visibility may increase the risk of an accident, possibly causing occupants or other road users to be injured if immediate evasive action is not taken by the driver.

All adverse weather conditions require the driver to *slow down* to accommodate the conditions and to avoid the risk of loss of control or possible collision. Assisted by the charted speed limits contained herein, the driver can slow down, remain physically and visually alert and prepare to decelerate further at all danger spots, possibly slowing to a complete stop beside the road if necessary until it is safe to proceed. A short wait or increased travelling time may avert years of heartache and suffering, and may spare other motorists the same.

This manual is intended to provide the reader with a

clear guide to follow when confronted with these and other situations, and includes suggested speed limits to assist the driver in negotiating danger spots more safely and with a reduced risk. These recommended speeds may not always be appropriate and suitable in the various zones and circumstances, and the reader may have to slow down further in situations as necessary in order to maintain an acceptable level of travel safety. Charted evasive action to be taken by the driver when approaching danger spots and charted appropriate action to be taken when road surfaces and weather conditions change are intended to improve driver and passenger safety at all times.

Reduced Visibility Conditions

SUNLIGHT GLARE: slow to 20 kph below the limit and prepare to stop immediately if necessary

RAIN/DRIZZLE: slow to 20 kph below the limit and proceed cautiously

SMOKE: slow to 30 kph below the limit and proceed with caution

FOG: slow to 30 kph below limit and proceed cautiously

SMOG: slow to 20 kph or more below limit and proceed carefully

Altered Road Conditions

RAIN/DRIZZLE: slow to 10 kph below the limit and proceed cautiously

SLEET: slow to 20 kph, stopping if necessary

MUD: slow to 20 kph, stopping if necessary

DEBRIS/SAND: slow to 20 kph and proceed with caution

BULL DUST: slow to 40 kph and proceed cautiously

FUEL OR OIL: slow to 30 kph and avoid the spillage, then exit the area

WATER ON THE ROAD: slow to 30 kph and proceed cautiously

NARROW ACCESS ROADS: slow to 30 kph and proceed cautiously

UN-LEVEL CORNERS: slow to 40 kph below the limit and proceed cautiously

Definitions

DRIVER'S SAFETY:	refers to the safe, calm and relaxed arrival of the driver and vehicle at the chosen destination, and their safe return
DANGER SPOT:	refers to a point along the way associated statistically with fatalities resulting from collisions at this point
SPEED:	refers to speeds well below the declared limits. Always ensure that the vehicle is kept at least 2 metres from all other objects
NON-RESIDENTIAL:	open roads with limited access and major thoroughfares and routes
SEMI-RESIDENTIAL:	roads with unlimited access and restricted limits
RESIDENTIAL:	local and city roads with restricted limits
ROAD CONDITION:	refers to surface condition and

shape of the road

DAY DRY:	daylight, dry weather
NIGHT DRY:	night, dry weather
DAY WET:	daylight, wet weather
NIGHT WET:	night, wet weather
CAR AND FWD:	includes passenger cars, four-wheel-drives, light trucks, vans and utility vehicles
TRUCK AND BUS:	includes dual wheel, tandem and tri-axle trucks and articulated vehicles, and all passenger-carrying buses
MOTORCYCLE:	includes on- and off-road motorcycles, sidecars and trikes
SIGNPOSTED:	refers to designated signposted speed limits
UNSIGNPOSTED:	refers to roads with no signposted limits or limits clearly unreasonable for the road conditions

DANGER SPOTS ON ROADS

All roads have danger spots where the majority of fatal accidents occur, regardless of efforts by the authorities to curb the risk.

DANGER SPOTS are, in order of importance:

- 'T' INTERSECTIONS
- CROSS and '+' INTERSECTIONS
- colliding with PASSING ONCOMING VEHICLES and while OVERTAKING VEHICLES
- colliding with OBJECTS and PEDESTRIANS on or near the road
- REAR-END, SIDE-ANGLE and SIDE-SWIPE collisions including colliding while STOPPING, LANE-CHANGING, MERGING and LEAVING
- colliding on and into BRIDGES and CAUSEWAYS
- 'Y' and ROUNDABOUT INTERSECTIONS
- when vehicles ROLL OVER on CORNERS
- colliding with TRAINS on RAIL LINES

DECELERATE HERE AND BE VERY ALERT

At 'T' INTERSECTIONS: slow to 30 kph below the limit and approach the intersection visually alert and physically ready and able to stop, only proceeding when safe to do so

At CROSS and '+' INTERSECTIONS: slow to 30 kph below

the limit and approach the intersection visually alert and physically able to stop, proceeding when safe

When passing ON-COMING vehicles and OVERTAKING vehicles: slow to 20 kph below the limit and proceed when safe

When OBJECTS or PEDESTRIANS are on or near the road: slow to 40 kph below the limit and proceed if and when safe to do so

Where REAR-END, SIDE-ANGLE and SIDE-SWIPE collisions may occur: slow to 20 kph below the limit and proceed when safe

When approaching BRIDGES and CAUSEWAYS: slow to 20 kph below the limit and proceed if and when safe to do so

At 'Y' and ROUNDABOUT INTERSECTIONS: slow to 30 kph below the limit and approach the intersection visually ready and physically able to stop, only proceeding when safe

On CORNERS and UN-LEVEL ROADS where a risk of ROLL-OVER exists: slow to 40 kph below the limit and proceed cautiously if and when safe to do so or slow further

At RAIL LINE LEVEL-CROSSINGS: slow to 30 kph and look in both directions well before crossing the line, remaining physically prepared to stop if necessary. Do not rely on the lights, gates or train whistle to alert you to the danger, and only proceed when safe to do so

Areas to Avoid

Dangerous intersections on narrow roads, hills, corners, rises and valleys and roads with poor visibility should be avoided if possible. Also avoid the following if possible:

overtaking procedures and narrow roads; where objects such as trees, posts, concrete barriers and parked cars are on or are very near the street, creating a possible risk to safety; crossing narrow bridges and causeways; roads which are un-level or uneven, with sharp or awkward corners where a possibility of roll-over exists or where the risk is increased; streets which cross railway lines or where heavy rail traffic crosses the road.

Other Risk Areas

Most other road fatalities occurring outside the danger spot areas happen as a result of people falling underneath vehicles from bicycles and motorcycles; falling from vehicles; being struck by items or loads falling from vehicles and colliding with animals. Other fatalities occur as a result or combination of: driver illness or distraction; unfitted seat belts; speeding; and mechanical failure.

Cyclists and Pedestrians

Watch out for cyclists, and when approaching them slow to 20 kph below the limit to reduce and avoid the possibility of a collision. Always watch for pedestrians on or near the road and when approaching them slow to 40 kph below the limit to ensure safety. If weather or road conditions are unfavourable, reduce vehicle speeds significantly further.

Motorcyclists

Always watch out for motorcyclists as they can be harder to see and may be speeding. Motorists may be required to take immediate evasive action, which may involve decelerating or merely applying additional caution when a motorcycle is near.

Lights, Horn, Hazard Lights and Indicator Applications

Switch on the DRIVING LIGHTS whenever weather conditions limit visibility in any way whatsoever or limit the visibility of other drivers. This may be during the day, in the evening, afternoon, morning and at all other times of low light or low vision.

Use the HORN if necessary to alert pedestrians or cyclists when they are crossing or near the road; where children are near the road; or if necessary where road works are in progress to alert the workmen.

Switch on the HAZARD LIGHTS whenever necessary to alert other drivers of any present dangerous predicament or when you wish to slow your vehicle down significantly or stop it.

Use the INDICATOR well before changing directions to alert other motorists of your intentions, always bearing in mind that they may not notice or may not be aware of your intentions, possibly requiring that immediate evasive action be taken to ensure safety.

Road Works in Progress or Recent Maintenance

When approaching areas where road works are in progress slow to 30 kph, preparing to stop if necessary. Loose stones or a loose surface after repairs may lead to glass damage and may decrease braking ability. To compensate and to ensure safety, slow to 30 kph and proceed with caution.

At Kindergartens, Schools and Gatherings of Children or Adults and Near Buses

Slow to 30 kph and proceed cautiously, remaining visually alert and physically able to stop if necessary. Avoid driving aggressively and always consider safety before and during each road journey. Readily permit faster motorists following behind to pass by slowing down gradually and moving over slightly if safe to do so.

CONDITION
SUGGESTIONS

The following suggestions outline the maximum speeds the author recommends when travelling in various weather and road conditions. Cars and four-wheel-drives have been placed together, as have trucks and buses, while motorcycles have been individually mentioned. The five different road conditions mentioned are adequate; narrow; unsealed; track and all other.

ADEQUATE: refers to national highways and multi-lane freeways which are wide, sealed and line marked

NARROW: refers to main roads which link towns and cities but are usually narrower, and either not line-marked or poorly line-marked, and usually are in poor condition with more corners, bridges and hills than the national highways

UNSEALED: refers to unsealed main roads which link towns and cities and which are usually narrow but well maintained

TRACK: refers to narrow, unsealed, under-maintained roads and off-road tracks which access remote areas

ALL OTHER: refers to all other narrow and
                          winding roads which require the
                          driver to slow down even further
                          to maintain safety

These conditions are mentioned in the Non-Residential,
Semi-Residential and Residential sections.

NON-RESIDENTIAL: areas with signposted limits of
                          100 kph, 110 kph or more

SEMI-RESIDENTIAL: areas with signposted limits of
                          80 kph

RESIDENTIAL: areas with signposted limits of
                          60 kph

'l' refers to light rain, 'm' to medium rain, and 'h' to
heavy rain.

In areas where the signposted speed limits are different to those stated in the charts, the author urges the
reader to adhere to reduced speeds equivalent to those
stated in the various charts and suggestions. Driving at
speeds below the signposted speed limits is one of the
cornerstones of achieving the levels of safety intended
by this manual. At these reduced speeds, clearly aware
of where the danger spots are and with charted views on
how to negotiate these areas more safely, the driver can
travel more confidently in all weather conditions and on
all road conditions. The driver may then achieve a
significantly higher level of road safety.

Non-Residential Areas – Conditions and Speeds

CAR AND FWD – DAY DRY CONDITIONS

Day Dry Driving on Adequate Road (Multi-Lane Freeways) – 100 kph or 110 kph

When driving a car or FWD on a road which is wide, smooth, straight, flat and in good condition and the recommended speed is 100 kph or 110 kph, proceed cautiously at a speed of 90 kph.

Day Dry Driving on Narrow, Rough or Winding Road (Country Main Roads) – 100 kph

When driving a car or FWD on a road which is narrow, rough or has high shoulders where the bitumen drops off sharply and the recommended speed is 100 kph, proceed cautiously at a speed of 80 kph.

Day Dry Driving on Unsealed Road – 100 kph

When driving a car or FWD on a gravel road that is wide, smooth, straight, flat and in good condition and the recommended speed is 100 kph, proceed cautiously at a speed of 70 kph.

Day Dry Driving on Narrow, Rough or Winding Track Road – Un-Signposted or 100 kph

When driving a car or FWD on a dirt road which is narrow, rough, drops off sharply into the drain or has large potholes and the recommended speed is 100 kph, proceed cautiously at a speed of 60 kph.

Day Dry Driving on All Other Narrow, Rough or Winding Access Roads Including One-Lane Roads – Un-Signposted

When driving a car or FWD during the day on any access road which is narrow, rough or winding, proceed cautiously at a speed of 40 kph.

CAR AND FWD – NIGHT DRY CONDITIONS

Night Dry Driving on Adequate Road (Multi-Lane Freeways) – 100 kph or 110 kph

When driving a car or FWD at night on a road which is wide, smooth, straight, flat and in good condition and the recommended speed is 100 kph or 110 kph, proceed cautiously at a speed of 85 kph.

Night Dry Driving on Narrow, Rough or Winding Road (Country Main Roads) – 100 kph

When driving a car or FWD at night on a road which is narrow, rough or has high shoulders and the bitumen drops off sharply and the recommended speed is 100 kph, proceed cautiously at a speed of 75 kph.

Night Dry Driving on Unsealed Road – 100 kph

When driving a car or FWD at night on a gravel road which is wide, smooth, straight, flat and in good condition and the recommended speed is 100 kph, proceed cautiously at a speed of 65 kph.

Night Dry Driving on Narrow, Rough or Winding Track Road – Un-Signposted or 100 kph

When driving a car or FWD at night on a dirt road which is narrow, rough, drops off sharply into the drain or has large potholes and the recommended speed is 100 kph, proceed cautiously at a speed of 55 kph.

Night Dry Driving on All Other Narrow, Rough or Winding Access Roads Including One-Lane Roads – Un-Signposted

When driving a car or FWD at night on any access road which is narrow, rough or winding, proceed cautiously at a speed of 40 kph.

CAR AND FWD – DAY WET CONDITIONS

Day Wet Driving on Adequate Road (Multi-Lane Freeways) – 100 kph or 110 kph

When driving a car or FWD on a wet road which is wide, smooth, straight, flat and in good condition and the recommended speed is 100 kph or 110 kph, proceed cautiously at a speed of 85 kph-l, 80-m, 75-h.*

Day Wet Driving on Narrow, Rough or Winding Road (Country Main Roads) – 100 kph

When driving a car or FWD on a wet road which is narrow, rough, or has high shoulders and the bitumen drops off sharply and the recommended speed is 100 kph, proceed cautiously at a speed of 75 kph, 70, 65.

Day Wet Driving on Unsealed Road – 100 kph

When driving a car or FWD on a wet gravel road which is wide, smooth, straight, flat and in good condition and the recommended speed is 100 kph, proceed cautiously at a speed of 65 kph, 60, 55.

Day Wet Driving on Narrow, Rough or Winding Track Road – Un-Signposted or 100 kph

When driving a car or FWD on a wet dirt road which is narrow, rough, drops off sharply into the drain or has

---

* Where 'l' indicates light rain, 'm' medium and 'h' heavy.

large potholes and the recommended speed is 100 kph, proceed cautiously at a speed of 55 kph, 50, 45.

Day Wet Driving on All Other Narrow, Rough or Winding Access Roads Including One-Lane Roads – Un-Signposted

When driving a car or FWD on a wet access road which is narrow, rough or winding, proceed cautiously at a speed of 40 kph, 35, 30.

CAR AND FWD – NIGHT WET CONDITIONS

Night Wet Driving on Adequate Road (Multi-Lane Freeways) – 100 kph or 110 kph

When driving a car or FWD at night on a wet road which is wide, smooth, straight, flat and in good condition and the recommended speed is 100 kph or 110 kph, proceed cautiously at a speed of 80 kph-l, 75-m, 70-h.

Night Wet Driving on Narrow, Rough or Winding Road (Country Main Roads) – 100 kph

When driving a car or FWD at night on a wet road which is narrow, rough, or has high shoulders and the bitumen drops off sharply and the recommended speed is 100 kph, proceed cautiously at a speed of 70 kph, 65, 60.

Night Wet Driving on Unsealed Road – 100 kph

When driving a car or FWD at night on a gravel road which is wide, smooth, straight, flat and in good condition and the recommended speed is 100 kph, proceed cautiously at a speed of 60 kph, 55, 50.

Night Wet Driving on Narrow, Rough or Winding Track Road – Un-Signposted or 100 kph

When driving a car or FWD at night on a wet dirt road

which is narrow, rough, drops off sharply into the drain or has large potholes and the recommended speed is 100 kph, proceed cautiously at a speed of 50 kph, 45, 40.

Night Wet Driving on All Other Narrow, Rough or Winding Access Roads Including One-Lane Roads – Un-Signposted

When driving a car or FWD at night on a wet access road which is narrow, rough or winding, proceed cautiously at a speed of 35 kph, 30, 25.

TRUCK AND BUS – DAY DRY CONDITIONS

Day Dry Driving on Adequate Road (Multi-Lane Freeways) – 100 kph or 110 kph

When driving a truck or bus on a road which is wide, smooth, straight, flat and in good condition and the recommended speed is 100 kph or 110 kph, proceed cautiously at a speed of 85 kph.

Day Dry Driving on Narrow, Rough or Winding Road (Country Main Roads) – 100 kph

When driving a truck or bus at night on a road which is narrow, rough, or has high shoulders and the bitumen drops off sharply and the recommended speed is 100 kph, proceed cautiously at a speed of 75 kph.

Day Dry Driving on Unsealed Road – 100 kph

When driving a truck or bus on a gravel road which is wide, smooth, straight, flat and in good condition and the recommended speed is 100 kph, proceed cautiously at a speed of 65 kph.

Day Dry Driving on Narrow, Rough or Winding Track Road – Un-Signposted or 100 kph

When driving a truck or bus on a dirt road which is narrow, rough, drops off sharply into the drain or has large potholes and the recommended speed is 100 kph, proceed cautiously at a speed of 55 kph.

Day Dry Driving on All Other Narrow, Rough or Winding Access Roads Including One-Lane Roads – Un-Signposted

When driving a truck or bus on any access road which is narrow, rough or winding, proceed cautiously at a speed of 40 kph.

TRUCK AND BUS – NIGHT DRY CONDITIONS

Night Dry Driving on Adequate Road (Multi-Lane Freeways) – 100 kph or 110 kph

When driving a truck or bus at night on a road which is wide, smooth, straight, flat and in good condition and the recommended speed is 100 kph or 110 kph, proceed cautiously at a speed of 80 kph.

Night Dry Driving on Narrow, Rough or Winding Road (Country Main Roads) – 100 kph

When driving a truck or bus on a road which is narrow, rough, or has high shoulders and the bitumen drops off sharply and the recommended speed is 100 kph, proceed cautiously at a speed of 70 kph.

Night Dry Driving on Unsealed Road – 100 kph

When driving a truck or bus at night on a gravel road which is wide, smooth, straight, flat and in good condition and the recommended speed is 100 kph, proceed cautiously at a speed of 60 kph.

Night Dry Driving on Narrow, Rough or Winding Track Road – Un-Signposted or 100 kph

When driving a truck or bus at night on a dirt road which is narrow, rough, drops off sharply into the drain or has large potholes and the recommended speed is 100 kph, proceed cautiously at a speed of 50 kph.

Night Dry Driving on All Other Narrow, Rough or Winding Access Roads Including One-Lane Roads – Un-Signposted

When driving a truck or bus at night on any access road which is narrow, rough or winding, proceed cautiously at a speed of 40 kph.

TRUCK AND BUS – DAY WET CONDITIONS

Day Wet Driving on Adequate Road (Multi-Lane Freeways) – 100 kph or 110 kph

When driving a truck or bus on a wet road which is wide, smooth, straight, flat and in good condition and the recommended speed is 100 kph or 110 kph, proceed cautiously at a speed of 80 kph-l, 75-m, 70-h.

Day Wet Driving on Narrow, Rough or Winding Road (Country Main Roads) – 100 kph

When driving a truck or bus on a wet road which is narrow, rough, or has high shoulders and the bitumen drops off sharply and the recommended speed is 100 kph, proceed cautiously at a speed of 70 kph, 65, 60.

Day Wet Driving on Unsealed Road – 100 kph

When driving a truck or bus on a wet gravel road which is wide, smooth, straight, flat and in good condition and the recommended speed is 100 kph, proceed cautiously at a speed of 60 kph, 55, 50.

Day Wet Driving on Narrow, Rough or Winding Track Road – Un-Signposted or 100 kph

When driving a truck or bus on a wet dirt road which is narrow, rough, drops off sharply into the drain or has large potholes and the recommended speed is 100 kph, proceed cautiously at a speed of 50 kph, 45, 40.

Day Wet Driving on All Other Narrow, Rough or Winding Access Roads Including One-Lane Roads – Un-Signposted

When driving a truck or bus on a wet access road which is narrow, rough or winding, proceed cautiously at a speed of 40 kph, 35, 30.

TRUCK AND BUS – NIGHT WET CONDITIONS

Night Wet Driving on Adequate Road (Multi-Lane Freeways) – 100 kph or 110 kph

When driving a truck or bus at night on a wet road which is wide, smooth, straight, flat and in good condition and the recommended speed is 100 kph or 110 kph, proceed cautiously at a speed of 75 kph-l, 70-m, 65-h.

Night Wet Driving on Narrow, Rough or Winding Road (Country Main Roads) – 100 kph

When driving a truck or bus at night on a wet road which is narrow, rough, or has high shoulders and the bitumen drops off sharply and the recommended speed is 100 kph, proceed cautiously at a speed of 65 kph, 60, 55.

Night Wet Driving on Unsealed Road – 100 kph

When driving a truck or bus at night on a wet gravel road which is wide, smooth, straight, flat and in good condition and the recommended speed is 100 kph, proceed cautiously at a speed of 55 kph, 50, 45.

Night Wet Driving on Narrow, Rough or Winding Track Road – Un-Signposted or 100 kph

When driving a truck or bus at night on a wet dirt road which is narrow, rough, drops off sharply into the drain or has large potholes and the recommended speed is 100 kph, proceed cautiously at a speed of 45 kph, 40, 35.

Night Wet Driving on All Other Narrow, Rough or Winding Access Roads Including One-Lane Roads – Un-Signposted

When driving a truck or bus at night on a wet access road which is narrow, rough or winding, proceed cautiously at a speed of 40 kph, 35, 30.

MOTORCYCLE – DAY DRY CONDITIONS

Day Dry Riding on Adequate Road (Multi-Lane Freeways) – 100 kph or 110 kph

When riding a motorcycle on a road which is wide, smooth, straight, flat and in good condition and the recommended speed is 100 kph or 110 kph, proceed cautiously at a speed of 80 kph.

Day Dry Riding on Narrow, Rough or Winding Road (Country Main Roads) – 100 kph

When riding a motorcycle on a road which is narrow, rough, or has high shoulders and the bitumen drops off sharply and the recommended speed is 100 kph, proceed cautiously at a speed of 70 kph.

Day Dry Riding on Unsealed Road – 100 kph

When riding a motorcycle on a gravel road which is wide, smooth, straight, flat and in good condition and the recommended speed is 100 kph, proceed cautiously at a speed of 60 kph.

Day Dry Riding on Narrow, Rough or Winding Track Road – Un-Signposted or 100 kph

When riding a motorcycle on a dirt road which is narrow, rough, drops off sharply into the drain or has large potholes and the recommended speed is 100 kph, proceed cautiously at a speed of 50 kph.

Day Dry Riding on All Other Narrow, Rough or Winding Access Roads Including One-Lane Roads – Un-Signposted

When riding a motorcycle on an access road which is narrow, rough or winding, proceed cautiously at a speed of 40 kph.

MOTORCYCLE – NIGHT DRY CONDITIONS

Night Dry Riding on Adequate Road (Multi-Lane Freeways) – 100 kph or 110 kph

When riding a motorcycle at night on a road which is wide, smooth, straight, flat and in good condition and the recommended speed is 100 kph or 110 kph, proceed cautiously at a speed of 75 kph.

Night Dry Riding on Narrow, Rough or Winding Road (Country Main Roads) – 100 kph

When riding a motorcycle at night on a road which is narrow, rough, or has high shoulders and the bitumen drops off sharply and the recommended speed is 100 kph, proceed cautiously at a speed of 65 kph.

Night Dry Riding on Unsealed Road – 100 kph

When riding a motorcycle at night on a gravel road which is wide, smooth, straight, flat and in good condition and the recommended speed is 100 kph, proceed cautiously at a speed of 55 kph.

Night Dry Riding on Narrow, Rough or Winding Track Road – Un-Signposted or 100 kph

When riding a motorcycle at night on a dirt road which is narrow, rough, drops off sharply into the drain or has large potholes and the recommended speed is 100 kph, proceed cautiously at a speed of 45 kph.

Night Dry Riding on All Other Narrow, Rough or Winding Access Roads Including One-Lane Roads – Un-Signposted

When riding a motorcycle at night on an access road which is narrow, rough or winding, proceed cautiously at a speed of 35 kph.

MOTORCYCLE – DAY WET CONDITIONS

Day Wet Riding on Adequate Road (Multi-Lane Freeways) – 100 kph

When riding a motorcycle on a wet road which is wide, smooth, straight, flat and in good condition and the recommended speed is 100 kph, proceed cautiously at a speed of 75 kph-l, 70-m, 65-h.

Day Wet Riding on Narrow, Rough or Winding Road (Country Main Roads) – 100 kph

When riding a motorcycle on a wet road which is narrow, rough, or has high shoulders and the bitumen drops off sharply and the recommended speed is 100 kph, proceed cautiously at a speed of 65 kph, 60, 55.

Day Wet Riding on Unsealed Road – 100 kph

When riding a motorcycle on a wet gravel road which is wide, smooth, straight, flat and in good condition and the recommended speed is 100 kph, proceed cautiously at a speed of 55 kph, 50, 45.

Day Wet Riding on Narrow, Rough or Winding Track Road – Un-Signposted or 100 kph

When riding a motorcycle on a wet dirt road which is narrow, rough, drops off sharply into the drain or has large potholes and the recommended speed is 100 kph, proceed cautiously at a speed of 45 kph, 40, 35.

Day Wet Riding on All Other Narrow, Rough or Winding Access Roads Including One-Lane Roads – Un-Signposted

When riding a motorcycle on a wet access road which is narrow, rough or winding, proceed cautiously at a speed of 35 kph, 30, 25.

MOTORCYCLE – NIGHT WET CONDITIONS

Night Wet Riding on Adequate Road (Multi-Lane Freeways) – 100 kph or 110 kph

When riding a motorcycle at night on a wet road which is wide, smooth, straight, flat and in good condition and the recommended speed is 100 kph or 110 kph, proceed cautiously at a speed of 70 kph-l, 65-m, 60-h.

Night Wet Riding on Narrow, Rough or Winding Road (Country Main Roads) – 100 kph

When riding a motorcycle at night on a wet road which is narrow, rough, or has high shoulders and the bitumen drops off sharply and the recommended speed is 100 kph, proceed cautiously at a speed of 60 kph, 55, 50.

Night Wet Riding on Unsealed Road – 100 kph

When riding a motorcycle at night on a wet gravel road which is wide, smooth, straight, flat and in good condition and the recommended speed is 100 kph, proceed cautiously at a speed of 50 kph, 45, 40.

Night Wet Riding on Narrow, Rough or Winding Track Road – Un-Signposted or 100 kph

When riding a motorcycle at night on a wet dirt road which is narrow, rough, drops off sharply into the drain or has large potholes and the recommended speed is 100 kph, proceed cautiously at a speed of 40 kph, 35, 30.

Night Wet Riding on All Other Narrow, Rough or Winding Access Roads Including One-Lane Roads – Un-Signposted

When riding a motorcycle at night on a wet access road which is narrow, rough or winding, proceed cautiously at a speed of 30 kph, 25, 20.

Semi-Residential Areas – Conditions and Speeds

CAR AND FWD – DAY DRY CONDITIONS

Day Dry Driving on Adequate Road (Semi-Residential Area) – 80 kph

When driving a car or FWD on a road which is wide, smooth, straight, flat and in good condition and the recommended speed is 80 kph, proceed cautiously at a speed of 75 kph.

Day Dry Driving on Narrow, Rough or Winding Road (Semi-Residential Area) – 80 kph

When driving a car or FWD on a road which is narrow, rough, or has high shoulders where the bitumen drops off sharply and the recommended speed is 80 kph, proceed cautiously at a speed of 70 kph.

See page 58 for UNSEALED and TRACK

Day Dry Driving on All Other Narrow, Rough or Winding Access Roads Including One-Lane Roads – Un-Signposted

When driving a car or FWD on an access road which is narrow, rough or winding, proceed cautiously at a speed of 40 kph.

CAR AND FWD – NIGHT DRY CONDITIONS

Night Dry Driving on Adequate Road (Semi-Residential Area) – 80 kph

When driving a car or FWD at night on a road which is wide, smooth, straight, flat and in good condition and the recommended speed is 80 kph, proceed cautiously at a speed of 70 kph.

Night Dry Driving on Narrow, Rough or Winding Road (Semi-Residential Area) – 80 kph

When driving a car or FWD at night on a road which is narrow, rough, or has high shoulders where the bitumen drops off sharply and the recommended speed is 80 kph, proceed cautiously at a speed of 65 kph.

See page 58 for UNSEALED and TRACK

Night Dry Driving on All Other Narrow, Rough or Winding Access Roads Including One-Lane Roads – Un-Signposted

When driving a car or FWD at night on an access road which is narrow, rough or winding, proceed cautiously at a speed of 40 kph.

CAR AND FWD – DAY WET CONDITIONS

Day Wet Driving on Adequate Road (Semi-Residential Area) – 80 kph

When driving a car or FWD on a wet road which is wide, smooth, straight, flat and in good condition and the recommended speed is 80 kph, proceed cautiously at a speed of 70 kph-l, 65-m, 60-h.

Day Wet Driving on Narrow, Rough or Winding Road (Semi-Residential Area) – 80 kph

When driving a car or FWD on a wet road which is narrow, rough, or has high shoulders where the bitumen drops off sharply and the recommended speed is 80 kph, proceed cautiously at a speed of 65 kph, 60, 55.

See page 59 for UNSEALED and TRACK

Day Wet Driving on All Other Narrow, Rough or Winding Access Roads Including One-Lane Roads – Un-Signposted

When driving a car or FWD on a wet access road which is narrow, rough or winding, proceed cautiously at a speed of 40 kph-l, 35-m, 30-h.

CAR AND FWD – NIGHT WET CONDITIONS

Night Wet Driving on Adequate Road (Semi-Residential Area) – 80 kph

When driving a car or FWD at night on a wet road which is wide, smooth, straight, flat and in good condition and the recommended speed is 80 kph, proceed cautiously at a speed of 65 kph-l, 60-m, 55-h.

Night Wet Driving on Narrow, Rough or Winding Road (Semi-Residential Area) – 80 kph

When driving a car or FWD at night on a wet road which is narrow, rough, or has high shoulders where the bitumen drops off sharply and the recommended speed is 80 kph, proceed cautiously at a speed of 60 kph, 55, 50.

See page 59 for UNSEALED and TRACK

Night Wet Driving on All Other Narrow, Rough or Winding Access Roads Including One-Lane Roads – Un-Signposted

When driving a car or FWD at night on a wet access road which is narrow, rough or winding, proceed cautiously at a speed of 40 kph, 35, 30.

TRUCK AND BUS – DAY DRY CONDITIONS

Day Dry Driving on Adequate Road (Semi-Residential Area) – 80 kph

When driving a truck or bus on a road which is wide, smooth, straight, flat and in good condition and the recommended speed is 80 kph, proceed cautiously at a speed of 70 kph.

Day Dry Driving on Narrow, Rough or Winding Road (Semi-Residential Area) – 80 kph

When driving a truck or bus on a road which is narrow, rough, or has high shoulders and the bitumen drops off sharply and the recommended speed is 80 kph, proceed cautiously at a speed of 65 kph.

See page 58 for UNSEALED and TRACK

Day Dry Driving on All Other Narrow, Rough or Winding Access Roads Including One-Lane Roads – Un-Signposted

When driving a truck or bus on an access road which is narrow, rough or winding, proceed cautiously at a speed of 40 kph.

TRUCK AND BUS – NIGHT DRY CONDITIONS

Night Dry Driving on Adequate Road (Semi-Residential Area) – 80 kph

When driving a truck or bus at night on a road which is wide, smooth, straight, flat and in good condition and the recommended speed is 80 kph, proceed cautiously at a speed of 65 kph.

Night Dry Driving on Narrow, Rough or Winding Road (Semi-Residential Area) – 80 kph

When driving a truck or bus at night on a road which is narrow, rough, or has high shoulders and the bitumen drops off sharply and the recommended speed is 80 kph, proceed cautiously at a speed of 60 kph.

See page 58 for UNSEALED and TRACK

Night Dry Driving on All Other Narrow, Rough or Winding Access Roads Including One-Lane Roads – Un-Signposted

When driving a truck or bus at night on an access road which is narrow, rough or winding, proceed cautiously at a speed of 40 kph.

Truck and Bus – Day Wet Conditions

Day Wet Driving on Adequate Road (Semi-Residential Area) – 80 kph

When driving a truck or bus on a wet road which is wide, smooth, straight, flat and in good condition and the recommended speed is 80 kph, proceed cautiously at a speed of 65 kph-l, 60-m, 55-h.

Day Wet Driving on Narrow, Rough or Winding Road (Semi-Residential Area) – 80 kph

When driving a truck or bus on a wet road which is narrow, rough, or has high shoulders and the bitumen drops off sharply and the recommended speed is 80 kph, proceed cautiously at a speed of 60 kph, 55, 50.

See page 59 for UNSEALED and TRACK

Day Wet Driving on All Other Narrow, Rough or Winding Access Roads Including One-Lane Roads – Un-Signposted

When driving a truck or bus on a wet access road which is narrow, rough or winding, proceed cautiously at a speed of 40 kph-l, 35-m, 30-h.

Truck and Bus – Night Wet Conditions

Night Wet Driving on Adequate Road (Semi-Residential Area) – 80 kph

When driving a truck or bus at night on a wet road which is wide, smooth, straight, flat and in good condition and the recommended speed is 80 kph, proceed cautiously at a speed of 60 kph-l, 55-m, 50-h.

Night Wet Driving on Narrow, Rough or Winding Road (Semi-Residential Area) – 80 kph

When driving a truck or bus at night on a wet road which is narrow, rough, or has high shoulders and the bitumen drops off sharply and the recommended speed is 80 kph, proceed cautiously at a speed of 55 kph, 50, 45.

See page 59 for UNSEALED and TRACK

Night Wet Driving on All Other Narrow, Rough or Winding Access Roads Including One-Lane Roads – Un-Signposted

When driving a truck or bus at night on a wet access road which is narrow, rough or winding, proceed cautiously at a speed of 40 kph, 35, 30.

MOTORCYCLE – DAY DRY CONDITIONS

Day Dry Riding on Adequate Road (Semi-Residential Area) – 80 kph

When riding a motorcycle on a road which is wide, smooth, straight, flat and in good condition and the recommended speed is 80 kph, proceed cautiously at a speed of 65 kph.

Day Dry Riding on Narrow, Rough or Winding Road (Semi-Residential Area) – 80 kph

When riding a motorcycle on a road which is narrow, rough, or has high shoulders and the bitumen drops off sharply and the recommended speed is 80 kph, proceed cautiously at speed of 60 kph.

See page 58 for UNSEALED and TRACK

Day Dry Riding on All Other Narrow, Rough or Winding Access Roads Including One-Lane Roads – Un-Signposted

When riding a motorcycle on an access road which is narrow, rough or winding, proceed cautiously at a speed of 35 kph.

MOTORCYCLE – NIGHT DRY CONDITIONS

Night Dry Riding on Adequate Road (Semi-Residential Area) – 80 kph

When riding a motorcycle at night on a road which is wide, smooth, straight, flat and in good condition and the recommended speed is 80 kph, proceed cautiously at a speed of 60 kph.

Night Dry Riding on Narrow, Rough or Winding Road (Semi-Residential Area) – 80 kph

When riding a motorcycle at night on a road which is narrow, rough, or has high shoulders and the bitumen drops off sharply and the recommended speed is 80 kph, proceed cautiously at speed of 55 kph.

See page 58 for UNSEALED and TRACK

Night Dry Riding on All Other Narrow, Rough or Winding Access Roads Including One-Lane Roads – Un-Signposted

When riding a motorcycle at night on an access road which is narrow, rough or winding, proceed cautiously at a speed of 30 kph.

MOTORCYCLE – DAY WET CONDITIONS

Day Wet Riding on Adequate Road (Semi-Residential Area) – 80 kph

When riding a motorcycle on a wet road which is wide, smooth, straight, flat and in good condition and the recommended speed is 80 kph, proceed cautiously at a speed of 60 kph-l, 55-m, 50-h.

Day Wet Riding on Narrow, Rough or Winding Road (Semi-Residential Area) – 80 kph

When riding a motorcycle on a wet road which is narrow, rough, or has high shoulders and the bitumen drops off sharply and the recommended speed is 80 kph, proceed cautiously at speed of 55 kph, 50, 45.

See page 59 for UNSEALED and TRACK

Day Wet Riding on All Other Narrow, Rough or Winding Access Roads Including One-Lane Roads – Un-Signposted

When riding a motorcycle on a wet access road which is narrow, rough or winding, proceed cautiously at a speed of 30 kph-l, 25-m, 20-h.

MOTORCYCLE – NIGHT WET CONDITIONS

Night Wet Riding on Adequate Road (Semi-Residential Area) – 80 kph

When riding a motorcycle at night on a wet road which is wide, smooth, straight, flat and in good condition and the recommended speed is 80 kph, proceed cautiously at a speed of 55 kph-l, 50-m, 45-h.

Night Wet Riding on Narrow, Rough or Winding Road (Semi-Residential Area) – 80 kph

When riding a motorcycle at night on a wet road which is narrow, rough, or has high shoulders and the bitumen drops off sharply and the recommended speed is 80 kph, proceed cautiously at a speed of 50 kph, 45, 40.

See page 59 for UNSEALED and TRACK

Night Wet Riding on All Other Narrow, Rough or Winding Access Roads Including One-Lane Roads – Un-Signposted

When riding a motorcycle at night on a wet access road which is narrow, rough or winding, proceed cautiously at a speed of 25 kph, 20, 15.

Residential Areas – Conditions and Speeds

CAR AND FWD – DAY DRY CONDITIONS

Day Dry Driving on Adequate Road (Residential Area) – 60 kph

When driving a car or FWD on a road which is wide, smooth, straight, flat and in good condition and the recommended speed is 60 kph, proceed cautiously at a speed of 55 kph.

Day Dry Driving on Narrow, Rough or Winding Road (Residential Area) – 60 kph

When driving a car or FWD on a road which is narrow, rough, or has high shoulders where the bitumen drops off sharply and the recommended speed is 60 kph, proceed cautiously at a speed of 50 kph.

See page 59 for UNSEALED and TRACK

Day Dry Driving on All Other Narrow, Rough or Winding Access Roads Including One-Lane Roads – Un-Signposted

When driving a car or FWD on an access road which is narrow, rough or winding, proceed cautiously at a speed of 35 kph.

CAR AND FWD – NIGHT DRY CONDITIONS

Night Dry Driving on Adequate Road (Residential Area) – 60 kph

When driving a car or FWD at night on a road which is wide, smooth, straight, flat and in good condition and the recommended speed is 60 kph, proceed cautiously at a speed of 50 kph.

Night Dry Driving on Narrow, Rough or Winding Road (Residential Area) – 60 kph

When driving a car or FWD at night on a road which is narrow, rough, or has high shoulders where the bitumen drops off sharply and the recommended speed is 60 kph, proceed cautiously at a speed of 45 kph.

See page 60 for UNSEALED and TRACK

CAR AND FWD – DAY WET CONDITIONS

Day Wet Driving on Adequate Road (Residential Area) – 60 kph

When driving a car or FWD on a wet road which is wide, smooth, straight, flat and in good condition and the recommended speed is 60 kph, proceed cautiously at a speed of 50 kph-l, 45-m, 40-h.

Day Wet Driving on Narrow, Rough or Winding Road (Residential Area) – 60 kph

When driving a car or FWD on a wet road which is narrow, rough, or has high shoulders where the bitumen drops off sharply and the recommended speed is 60 kph, proceed cautiously at a speed of 45 kph, 40, 35.

See page 60 for UNSEALED and TRACK

Day Wet Driving on All Other Narrow, Rough or Winding Access Roads Including One-Lane Roads – Un-Signposted

When driving a car or FWD on a wet access road which is narrow, rough or winding, proceed cautiously at a speed of 30 kph, 25, 20.

CAR AND FWD – NIGHT WET CONDITIONS

Night Wet Driving on Adequate Road (Residential Area) – 60 kph

When driving a car or FWD at night on a wet road which is wide, smooth, straight, flat and in good condition and the recommended speed is 60 kph, proceed cautiously at a speed of 45 kph-l, 40-m, 35-h.

Night Wet Driving on Narrow, Rough or Winding Road (Residential Area) – 60 kph

When driving a car or FWD at night on a wet road which is narrow, rough, or has high shoulders where the bitumen drops off sharply and the recommended speed is 60 kph, proceed cautiously at a speed of 40 kph, 35, 30.

See page 60 for UNSEALED and TRACK

TRUCK AND BUS – DAY DRY CONDITIONS

Day Dry Driving on Adequate Road (Residential Area) – 60 kph

When driving a truck or bus on a road which is wide, smooth, straight, flat and in good condition and the recommended speed is 60 kph, proceed cautiously at a speed of 50 kph.

Day Dry Driving on Narrow, Rough or Winding Road (Residential Area) – 60 kph

When driving a truck or bus on a road which is narrow, rough, or has high shoulders where the bitumen drops off sharply and the recommended speed is 60 kph, proceed cautiously at a speed of 45 kph.

See page 59 for UNSEALED and TRACK

TRUCK AND BUS – NIGHT DRY CONDITIONS

Night Dry Driving on Adequate Road (Residential Area) – 60 kph

When driving a truck or bus at night on a road which is wide, smooth, straight, flat and in good condition and the recommended speed is 60 kph, proceed cautiously at a speed of 45 kph.

Night Dry Driving on Narrow, Rough or Winding Road (Residential Area) – 60 kph

When driving a truck or bus at night on a road which is narrow, rough, or has high shoulders and the bitumen drops off sharply and the recommended speed is 60 kph, proceed cautiously at a speed of 40 kph.

See page 60 for UNSEALED and TRACK

TRUCK AND BUS – DAY WET CONDITIONS

Day Wet Driving on Adequate Road (Residential Area) – 60 kph

When driving a truck or bus on a wet road which is wide, smooth, straight, flat and in good condition and the recommended speed is 60 kph, proceed cautiously at a speed of 45 kph-l, 40-m, 35-h.

Day Wet Driving on Narrow, Rough or Winding Road (Residential Area) – 60 kph

When driving a truck or bus on a wet road which is narrow, rough, or has high shoulders and the bitumen drops off sharply and the recommended speed is 60 kph, proceed cautiously at a speed of 40 kph, 35, 30.

See page 60 for UNSEALED and TRACK

TRUCK AND BUS – NIGHT WET CONDITIONS

Night Wet Driving on Adequate Road (Residential Area) – 60 kph

When driving a truck or bus at night on a wet road which is wide, smooth, straight, flat and in good condition and the recommended speed is 60 kph, proceed cautiously at a speed of 40 kph-l, 35-m, 30-h.

Night Wet Driving on Narrow, Rough or Winding Road (Residential Area) – 60 kph

When driving a truck or bus at night on a wet road which is narrow, rough, or has high shoulders and the bitumen drops off sharply and the recommended speed is 60 kph, proceed cautiously at a speed of 35 kph, 30, 25.

See page 60 for UNSEALED and TRACK

MOTORCYCLE – DAY DRY CONDITIONS

Day Dry Riding on Adequate Road (Residential Area) – 60 kph

When riding a motorcycle on a road which is wide, smooth, straight, flat and in good condition and the recommended speed is 60 kph, proceed cautiously at a speed of 45 kph.

Day Dry Riding on Narrow, Rough or Winding Road (Residential Area) – 60 kph

When riding a motorcycle on a road which is narrow, rough, or has high shoulders and the bitumen drops off sharply and the recommended speed is 60 kph, proceed cautiously at a speed of 40 kph.

See page 59 for UNSEALED and TRACK

MOTORCYCLE – NIGHT DRY CONDITIONS

Night Dry Riding on Adequate Road (Residential Area) – 60 kph

When riding a motorcycle at night on a road which is wide, smooth, straight, flat and in good condition and the recommended speed is 60 kph, proceed cautiously at a speed of 40 kph.

Night Dry Riding on Narrow, Rough or Winding Road (Residential Area) – 60 kph

When riding a motorcycle at night on a road which is narrow, rough, or has high shoulders and the bitumen drops off sharply and the recommended speed is 60 kph, proceed cautiously at a speed of 35 kph.

See page 60 for UNSEALED and TRACK

MOTORCYCLE – DAY WET CONDITIONS

Day Wet Riding on Adequate Road (Residential Area) – 60 kph

When riding a motorcycle on a wet road which is wide, smooth, straight, flat and in good condition and the recommended speed is 60 kph, proceed cautiously at a speed of 40 kph-l, 35-m, 30-h.

Day Wet Riding on Narrow, Rough or Winding Road (Residential Area) – 60 kph

When riding a motorcycle on a wet road which is narrow, rough, or has high shoulders and the bitumen drops off sharply and the recommended speed is 60 kph, proceed cautiously at a speed of 35 kph, 30, 25.

See page 60 for UNSEALED and TRACK

MOTORCYCLE – NIGHT WET CONDITIONS

Night Wet Riding on Adequate Road (Residential Area) – 60 kph

When riding a motorcycle at night on a wet road which is wide, smooth, straight, flat and in good condition and the recommended speed is 60 kph, proceed cautiously at a speed of 35 kph-l, 30-m, 25-h.

Night Wet Riding on Narrow, Rough or Winding Road (Residential Area) – 60 kph

When riding a motorcycle at night on a wet road which is narrow, rough, or has high shoulders and the bitumen drops off sharply and the recommended speed is 60 kph, proceed cautiously at a speed of 30 kph, 25, 20.

See page 60 for UNSEALED and TRACK

CONDITIONS AND SPEED CHARTS

Non-Residential Areas

DAY DRY CONDITIONS (SIGNPOSTED AT 100 KPH OR 110 KPH)

ROAD CONDITIONS	CAR AND FWD	TRUCK AND BUS	MOTORCYCLE
Adequate	90 kph	85 kph	80 kph
Narrow	80	75	70
Unsealed	70	65	60
Track	60	55	50

NIGHT DRY CONDITIONS (SIGNPOSTED AT 100 KPH OR 110 KPH)

ROAD CONDITIONS	CAR AND FWD	TRUCK AND BUS	MOTORCYCLE
Adequate	85 kph	80 kph	75 kph
Narrow	75	70	65
Unsealed	65	60	55
Track	55	50	45

DAY WET CONDITIONS (SIGNPOSTED AT 100 KPH OR 110 KPH)

ROAD CONDITIONS	CAR AND FWD	TRUCK AND BUS	MOTORCYCLE
Adequate	85 kph	80 kph	75 kph

Narrow	75	70	65
Unsealed	65	60	55
Track	55	50	45

NIGHT WET CONDITIONS (SIGNPOSTED AT 100 KPH OR 110 KPH)

ROAD CONDITIONS	CAR AND FWD	TRUCK AND BUS	MOTORCYCLE
Adequate	80 kph	75 kph	70 kph
Narrow	70	65	60
Unsealed	60	55	50
Track	50	45	40

Semi-Residential Areas

DAY DRY CONDITIONS (SIGNPOSTED AT 80 KPH)

ROAD CONDITIONS	CAR AND FWD	TRUCK AND BUS	MOTORCYCLE
Adequate	75 kph	70 kph	65 kph
Narrow	70	65	60
Unsealed	65	60	45
Track	60	55	40

NIGHT DRY CONDITIONS (SIGNPOSTED AT 80 KPH)

ROAD CONDITIONS	CAR AND FWD	TRUCK AND BUS	MOTORCYCLE
Adequate	70 kph	65 kph	60 kph
Narrow	65	60	55
Unsealed	60	55	40
Track	55	50	35

Day Wet Conditions (signposted at 80 kph)

Road Conditions	Car and Fwd	Truck and Bus	Motorcycle
Adequate	70 kph	65 kph	60 kph
Narrow	65	60	55
Unsealed	60	55	40
Track	55	50	35

Night Wet Conditions (signposted at 80 kph)

Road Conditions	Car and Fwd	Truck and Bus	Motorcycle
Adequate	65 kph	60 kph	55 kph
Narrow	60	55	50
Unsealed	55	50	35
Track	50	45	30

Residential Areas

Day Dry Conditions (signposted at 60 kph)

Road Conditions	Car and Fwd	Truck and Bus	Motorcycle
Adequate	55 kph	50 kph	45 kph
Narrow	50	45	40
Unsealed	45	40	35
Track	40	35	30

Night Dry Conditions (signposted at 60 kph)

Road Conditions	Car and Fwd	Truck and Bus	Motorcycle
Adequate	50 kph	45 kph	40 kph
Narrow	45	40	35

| Unsealed | 40 | 35 | 30 |
| Track | 35 | 30 | 25 |

DAY WET CONDITIONS (SIGNPOSTED AT 60 KPH)

ROAD CONDITIONS	CAR AND FWD	TRUCK AND BUS	MOTORCYCLE
Adequate	50 kph	45 kph	40 kph
Narrow	45	40	35
Unsealed	40	35	30
Track	35	30	25

NIGHT WET CONDITIONS (SIGNPOSTED AT 60 KPH)

ROAD CONDITIONS	CAR AND FWD	TRUCK AND BUS	MOTORCYCLE
Adequate	45 kph	40 kph	35 kph
Narrow	40	35	30
Unsealed	35	30	25
Track	30	25	20

Chart References

In the Danger Spot Speed Charts that follow, 'T',
'CROSS', 'Y' and 'RNDABTS' are intersections of these
types, and '+' are five-way or more mergings. 'OCMG'
and 'OTKG' are passing oncoming vehicles and overtaking vehicles. 'OBJECTS' are parked vehicles, buildings,
trees, barriers and pedestrians on or near the road.
'REAR' and 'SIDE' are rear and side collisions, occurring
while stopping, lane changing, merging and leaving.
'BRIDGES' are narrow bridges, causeways, grids and

tunnels. 'CORNERS' are all corners and un-level roads where a risk of roll over exists. 'RAIL LINES' are all rail line level crossings.

DANGER SPOT SPEED CHARTS

Non-Residential Areas

DAY DRY CONDITIONS (SIGNPOSTED AT 100 KPH OR 110 KPH)

DANGER SPOTS	CAR AND FWD	TRUCK AND BUS	MOTORCYCLE
'T'	70 kph	65 kph	60 kph
'CROSS' AND '+'	70	65	60
'OCMG' AND 'OTKG'	80	75	70
'OBJECTS'	60	55	50
'REAR' AND 'SIDE'	80	75	70
'BRIDGES'	80	75	70
'Y' AND 'RNDABTS'	70	65	60
'CORNERS'	60	55	50
'RAIL LINES'	30	25	20

NIGHT DRY CONDITIONS (SIGNPOSTED AT 100 KPH OR 110 KPH)

DANGER SPOTS	CAR AND FWD	TRUCK AND BUS	MOTORCYCLE
'T'	65 kph	60 kph	55 kph
'CROSS' AND '+'	65	60	55
'OCMG' AND 'OTKG'	75	70	65
'OBJECTS'	65	50	45
'REAR' AND 'SIDE'	75	70	65
'BRIDGES'	75	70	65
'Y' AND 'RNDABTS'	65	60	55
'CORNERS'	55	50	45
'RAIL LINES'	25	20	15

DAY WET CONDITIONS (SIGNPOSTED AT 100 KPH OR 110 KPH)

DANGER SPOTS	CAR AND FWD	TRUCK AND BUS	MOTORCYCLE
'T'	65 kph	60 kph	55 kph
'CROSS' AND '+'	65	60	55
'OCMG' AND 'OTKG'	75	70	65
'OBJECTS'	65	50	45
'REAR' AND 'SIDE'	75	70	65
'BRIDGES'	75	70	65
'Y' AND 'RNDABTS'	65	60	55
'CORNERS'	55	50	45
'RAIL LINES'	25	20	15

NIGHT WET CONDITIONS (SIGNPOSTED AT 100 KPH OR 110 KPH)

DANGER SPOTS	CAR AND FWD	TRUCK AND BUS	MOTORCYCLE
'T'	60 kph	55 kph	50 kph
'CROSS' AND '+'	60	55	50
'OCMG' AND 'OTKG'	70	65	60
'OBJECTS'	50	45	40
'REAR' AND 'SIDE'	70	65	60
'BRIDGES'	70	65	60
'Y' AND 'RNDABTS'	60	55	50
'CORNERS'	50	45	40
'RAIL LINES'	20	15	10

Semi-Residential Areas – Danger Spot Speed Charts

DAY DRY CONDITIONS (SIGNPOSTED AT 80 KPH)

DANGER SPOTS	CAR AND FWD	TRUCK AND BUS	MOTORCYCLE
'T'	50 kph	45 kph	40 kph
'CROSS' AND '+'	50	45	40

'Ocmg' and 'Otkg'	60	55	50
'Objects'	40	35	30
'Rear' and 'Side'	60	55	50
'Bridges'	60	55	50
'Y' and 'Rndabts'	50	45	40
'Corners'	40	35	30
'Rail Lines'	30	25	20

Night Dry Conditions (signposted at 80 kph)

Danger Spots	Car and Fwd	Truck and Bus	Motorcycle
'T'	45 kph	40 kph	35 kph
'Cross' and '+'	45	40	35
'Ocmg' and 'Otkg'	55	50	45
'Objects'	35	30	25
'Rear' and 'Side'	55	50	45
'Bridges'	55	50	45
'Y' and 'Rndabts'	45	40	35
'Corners'	35	30	25
'Rail Lines'	25	20	15

Day Wet Conditions (signposted at 80 kph)

Danger Spots	Car and Fwd	Truck and Bus	Motorcycle
'T'	45 kph	40 kph	35 kph
'Cross' and '+'	45	40	35
'Ocmg' and 'Otkg'	55	50	45
'Objects'	35	30	25
'Rear' and 'Side'	55	50	45
'Bridges'	55	50	45
'Y' and 'Rndabts'	45	40	35
'Corners'	35	30	25
'Rail Lines'	25	20	15

NIGHT WET CONDITIONS (SIGNPOSTED AT 80 KPH)

DANGER SPOTS	CAR AND FWD	TRUCK AND BUS	MOTORCYCLE
'T'	40 kph	35 kph	30 kph
'CROSS' AND '+'	40	35	30
'OCMG' AND 'OTKG'	50	45	40
'OBJECTS'	30	25	20
'REAR' AND 'SIDE'	50	45	40
'BRIDGES'	50	45	40
'Y' AND 'RNDABTS'	40	35	30
'CORNERS'	30	25	20
'RAIL LINES'	20	15	10

Residential Areas – Danger Spot Speed Charts

DAY DRY CONDITIONS (SIGNPOSTED AT 60 KPH)

DANGER SPOTS	CAR AND FWD	TRUCK AND BUS	MOTORCYCLE
'T'	30 kph	25 kph	20 kph
'CROSS' AND '+'	30	25	20
'OCMG' AND 'OTKG'	40	35	30
'OBJECTS'	20	15	10
'REAR' AND 'SIDE'	40	35	30
'BRIDGES'	40	35	30
'Y' AND 'RNDABTS'	30	25	20
'CORNERS'	20	15	10
'RAIL LINES'	20	15	10

NIGHT DRY CONDITIONS (SIGNPOSTED AT 60 KPH)

DANGER SPOTS	CAR AND FWD	TRUCK AND BUS	MOTORCYCLE
'T'	25 kph	20 kph	15 kph
'CROSS' AND '+'	25	20	15

LaVergne, TN USA
12 December 2009
166765LV00010B/2/A